Born in 1950, Rowan Williams was educated in Swansea (Wales) and Cambridge. He studied for his theology doctorate in Oxford, after which he taught theology in a seminary near Leeds. From 1977 until 1986, he was engaged in academic and parish work in Cambridge, before returning to Oxford as Lady Margaret Professor of Divinity. In 1990 he became a Fellow of the British Academy.

In 1992 Professor Williams became Bishop of Monmouth, and in 1999 he was elected as Archbishop of Wales. He became Archbishop of Canterbury in late 2002 with ten years' experience as a diocesan bishop and three as a primate in the Anglican Communion. As archbishop, his main responsibilities were pastoral – whether leading his own diocese of Canterbury and the Church of England, or guiding the Anglican Communion worldwide. At the end of 2012, after ten years as archbishop, he stepped down and moved to a new role as Master of Magdalene College, Cambridge.

Professor Williams is acknowledged internationally as an outstanding theological writer and teacher as well as an accomplished poet and translator. His interests include music, fiction and languages.

**Little Books of Guidance**
*Finding answers to life's big questions!*

Also in the series:

# WHAT IS CHRISTIANITY?

A little book of guidance

ROWAN WILLIAMS

First published in Great Britain in 2015

Society for Promoting Christian Knowledge
36 Causton Street
London SW1P 4ST
www.spck.org.uk

*British Library Cataloguing-in-Publication Data*
A catalogue record for this book is available from the British Library

ISBN 978–0–281–07439–6
eBook ISBN 978–0–281–07443–3

Typeset by Graphicraft Limited, Hong Kong
First printed in Great Britain by Ashford Colour Press
Subsequently digitally printed in Great Britain

eBook by Graphicraft Limited, Hong Kong

Produced on paper from sustainable forests

# Contents

# 1

## *What is Christianity all about?*

Imagine someone watching, over a period of about one year, the things that happen in a Christian church. They would be aware that one day of the week has special significance. Particularly if they are observing what happens in a historically Christian country, they would notice that Sunday is seen as important for meeting and praying. They would see that Christians meet to sing and speak to a God whom they describe as the maker of all things and the judge of all things, and that they kneel or bow in the presence of this God, thanking him and acknowledging their failures and sinfulness. They would see that extracts from a holy book are read in public and that instruction is given by leaders of the congregation in how to understand this book. They would perhaps notice that most of the prayers end with words referring to someone called Jesus Christ, and describing him as 'Lord'.

They would see that at different seasons Christians celebrate the birth of Jesus and also commemorate his death and his miraculous return from death. Sometimes they would hear prayers and blessings mentioning 'the Father, the Son and the Holy Spirit'. And finally, they would see that new members are brought into the community by a ceremony of pouring water on them or immersing them in water, and that the most regular action performed by communities of different kinds is the blessing and sharing of bread and wine. They would notice, perhaps with bewilderment or even shock, that this sharing of bread and wine is described as sharing the body and blood of Jesus.

In this little book, I am trying to think what questions might arise for someone looking at Christians from the outside in the way I have just imagined. These may or may not be the questions you have. But perhaps the attempt to answer these questions will help bring other questions more clearly into focus.

## *God: Father, Son and Holy Spirit*

Let me begin with the most obvious features of Christian prayer. We pray 'through Jesus Christ our Lord'. And the best known of all Christian prayers begins with the words 'Our Father in heaven'. These belong together. Probably the most important Christian belief is that we are given the right to speak to God in exactly the same way that Jesus did, because the life, the power, the Spirit that filled Jesus is given to us also.

We believe that Jesus, son of Mary, is fully a human being. But we believe more than that. Because of the divine authority that he shows in his power to teach and to forgive, as our Gospels describe it, we say also that the whole of his human life is the direct effect of God's action working in him at every moment. The image used by some Christian thinkers is that his human life is like iron that has been heated in the fire until it has the same power to burn as the fire does.

We call him the Son of God. But we do not mean by this that God is physically his father, or that he is made to be another God alongside the one God. We say rather that the one God is alive and real in three eternal and distinct ways. God is first the source of everything, the life from which everything flows out. But then we say that this one God is also living and real *in* that 'flowing-out'. The life that comes from him is not something different from him. It reflects all that he is. It shows his glory and beauty and communicates them. Christians say that God has a perfect and eternal 'image' of his glory, sometimes called his 'wisdom', sometimes called his 'Word', sometimes called his 'Son', though this is never to be understood in a physical and literal way. And we say that the one God, who is both source and outward-flowing life, who is both 'Father' and 'Son', is also active as the power that draws everything back to God, leading and guiding human beings – and indeed the whole universe – towards unity with the wisdom and goodness of God. This is the power we call 'Holy Spirit'.

So when we speak of 'the Father, the Son and the Holy Spirit', we do not at all mean to say that there are three gods – as if there were three divine people in heaven, like three human people in a room. Certainly we believe that the three ways in which God eternally exists and acts are distinct from one another – but not in the way that things in the world or even persons in the world are distinct. This is important in the context of dialogue with other faiths, not least with Islam: when Christians read in the Qur'an the strong condemnation of 'associating' with God other beings that are not God, they will agree wholeheartedly.

If we then return to what Christians believe about Jesus, perhaps we can see why they say that he is 'Son of God'. Because the eternal Word and wisdom of God completely occupies his human mind and body, we say that in him this Word and wisdom has 'become flesh', has been 'incarnated'. Just as the Word and wisdom eternally reflects God's glory and beauty, so in our human world, in human history, Jesus reflects this glory and beauty, showing us both the splendour of divine love and the true dignity and glory of humanity as God intends it to be. Because the Word and wisdom of God is sometimes described in the Jewish Scriptures of the Old Testament as a 'child' of God – and also because these Scriptures often call the kings of God's people who rule according to wisdom the 'sons of God' – we come to say that Jesus, who embodies God's wisdom and is anointed as ruler of God's people, is God's Son. And, as we have seen, from the very first, Christian thinkers have said that this language must not be thought of in any physical way.

When Jesus himself prays to God in his own human voice, he calls him 'Father'. And what we must now add to what we have said so far is that this title expresses not only the acknowledgement on the part of Jesus that his whole being comes directly from God, but also the trust and complete confidence that he enjoys with God. As the Gospel of St John tells us over and over again,

Jesus knows the very mind and heart of God and can reveal it completely and authoritatively to those he calls to be with him. When the Christian prays 'in the name of Jesus' and says 'Our Father', the Christian is saying to God: 'You have promised that, when I pray, you, O God, will hear the voice of Jesus, and you will look upon me with the same love that Jesus knew.' When we pray, we stand in the place of Jesus, we speak his words, and we hope in confidence that we shall receive the love he receives from the One he calls 'Father'.

## *Jesus: the Saviour*

Many who are not Christian think that this means Christians rely upon Jesus instead of trying to obey God's commands for themselves. Other faiths sometimes criticize Christians for treating human beings as if they were not fully responsible for their actions. But the Christian belief is this. When God created the world, he made all things according to his will. But the first human beings refused to obey God, although they knew what he asked of them. By rebelling against him in this way, they started a process of corruption in the world which spreads to everyone who is born into it. Even before a newborn child has learned to speak, it will have been touched and affected by a 'climate' of disobedience to God. We are all deeply affected by the actions of others, and sometimes we find that the results of other people's actions make it hard or even impossible to do what is right. Christians say that this is something that to some extent limits the

5

freedom of every human being. The purpose of God is there and it's plain enough in itself, but we are held in prison by this history of sin and disobedience. Such is the teaching of St Paul. This is what we mean when Christians sometimes speak of 'original sin' – the confusion and betrayal of God's purpose that is there in our world even before we have done anything.

Only God the creator can restore the freedom to live in a way that is in harmony with his will and his nature. How does he do this? When he creates Jesus in the womb of Mary, he brings into being a human life that will be perfectly obedient to his will because it is a human life completely filled with divine life – with the creative love and endless resourcefulness of God's own being. Jesus thus shows us what a human life is like when it is lived as it should be. But he does more than just *show* us. Because of his own perfect harmony with God's will and goodness, he is able to offer himself to rejection and death, so that by his death there may be a restored relationship of love between God and humanity. Christians say that Jesus, as he goes to the cross, accepts all the suffering that is the consequence for human beings of their rebellion and weakness. He 'pays the price' of human betrayal and weakness. Because he accepts this suffering as an act of love, he changes what is possible for human beings. They need no longer despair that they can never obey or love God.

When we come in trust to Jesus and identify with him, when we stand in his place and speak with his words, what happens, we believe, is that the Holy Spirit is giving us once again the freedom to live a life according to God's will, reflecting God's own character. Once we were not free, because the only kind of human fellowship or togetherness possible was 'togetherness' in the inheritance of disharmony and betrayal that affects us all. But Jesus creates a new kind of fellowship, a relationship with himself that is going to be stronger than the deep currents pulling us towards destructive and self-serving behaviour. St Paul says that this means there is a 'new creation'. We are able to start over again.

Christians have always found it hard to say exactly how this works. Some speak of Jesus taking the punishment for sin in our place; some speak of him offering himself as a sacrifice. Some speak of him winning a victory over Satan and setting all of us who are prisoners free. It seems that there is no one way of saying this correctly. But what matters is this. In the life of Jesus, the completeness of divine love breaks into a world in which human beings are not free and not in contact with that love. By approaching his death as an act of love for human beings, by speaking about it (as he does in the Gospels) as a sort of payment to the powers of evil that will release people from the effects of the sin of the first human beings, he 'opens the kingdom of heaven to all believers', to use the words of a very old Christian hymn.

And because God brings him back from death to meet again with his followers, we know that his life is not a thing of the past. He is still alive, eternally alive. He calls people to be with him just as he did in his life on earth. And so day by day he creates that community of fellowship with him which gives human beings the possibility of living differently, living in harmony with God. In the words of our Scriptures, he 'breathes' into his followers the power of the Holy Spirit, so that they are drawn back to God and God's ways. Because he rose from death 'on the first day of the week', according to the Gospels, Sunday has always been a special day for Christians. And the Easter season is the greatest of all Christian festivals.

When we receive the Holy Spirit, we still have to use our freedom to choose the good. But in fellowship with Jesus, we know that we have the help of the Spirit, giving us strength to resist temptation and wisdom to see where it lies. We also know that when we fail or fall back, as sometimes we are bound to do, the forgiving love of God will give us another opportunity to serve him, to try and model our lives on the life of Jesus and to let the freedom and love which he has planted in our hearts change all that we do and say. To ask for mercy and to rely on God's mercy does not let us off the obligation to use all our powers in God's service. They only assure us that, so long as we trust God, we shall be given fresh opportunities by his grace.

## *The Bible: God's written word*

When we read our holy book, the Bible, containing the Scriptures of the Jewish people (referred to by most Christians as the 'Old Testament') and also the writings of the first generation of believers in Jesus (the 'New Testament'), we do so in order to hear how God's revealing power has been at work in history. God's first actions to free human beings from the effects of the deep failure that happens at the very start of human history are to be seen in God's calling to Abraham to be the father of a people who will be close to God and know his purpose. Later God saves this nation from Egypt and, through the leadership of Moses, gives them a system of law that allows God's justice and mercy to shape the life of a whole community. The people of Israel experience a long history of both God's favour and God's judgement; and at last God sends Jesus as his Word, his gift, his action and presence in the world, so as to gather a people who will this time be not just one nation but a community of every nation – 'every tribe, people and language', as the New Testament says.

The books contained in the Bible are of very diverse character. Unlike the Qur'an, this is not a text delivered in a brief space of time to one person. The Bible is, we believe, a book that speaks with one voice about God and his will and nature; but it does so – to use a popular Christian image – like a *symphony* of different voices and instruments of music, miraculously held together in one story and one message about God, a story whose climax is Jesus. Sometimes parts of the Bible are hard to understand; sometimes different passages seem to contradict each other. This is not surprising when you remember that the books of the Bible were written over a period of more than a thousand years. But every word has been discussed and thought about for another two thousand years, and Christians have found that there is always a deep unity of thought, once it's agreed that the life of Jesus is the centre of the picture and that it makes sense of all the rest.

Traditionally, the first five books of the Bible, describing the creation, the flood, the history of Abraham and his family, the rescue of the people of Israel from Egypt and the giving of the law to Moses, are called the Pentateuch, the 'five books of Moses'. There are then books of historical chronicles, books of psalms and proverbs, the messages of the prophets who declared God's judgement against the people's falling away from justice and integrity and promised that God would restore them if they turned to him; and also a few books about how the people of Israel came back from their exile in Babylon. In the New Testament, the four Gospels ('gospel' means 'good news') tell the story of Jesus, the Acts of the Apostles tells of the spread of the faith, and the letters or 'epistles' of Paul, Peter, John, James and Jude are writings that give guidance on matters of belief and behaviour to different Christian communities. The Revelation to John is a vision of the last days of the world and the coming of Jesus in glory to judge all people.

Christians believe that the Bible is inspired by God – that is, they believe that the texts that make up the Bible were composed by the help of the Holy Spirit and that they communicate God's will perfectly when they are taken together and read in the context of prayer and worship. Some Christians believe that this means the Bible is never wrong about any statement of fact. Others, while agreeing that the Bible is the final authority, would say that this rather misunderstands the point of the Bible, which is not to give us infallible information about all sorts of things but to give a reliable guide to what God is like and so what will make for our own life and well-being.

In that sort of framework, we can see that the Bible doesn't need to be correct about every matter of fact – in the way ordinary human writers may be mistaken, about certain not very significant issues, about dates, about personal names or stories, about geography, and so on. We do not think that God *dictates* the Bible to its writers, but that he works with and in their human minds to communicate his purpose, to tell us what we need to know in order to be set free from our mistakes and sins.

Christians have spent much energy on the study of the Bible's texts and how they came to be composed. They have established the best evidence for the texts and have discovered and discussed very early examples of the manuscripts (we have a part of St John's Gospel on a piece of parchment dated less than a hundred years after Jesus). Sometimes the results of this study have been seen to be disturbing by those who insist upon the accuracy of every detail. But a large number of Christians accept the results of scholarly study as confirming the idea that the Bible tells one story in several different voices.

As the pattern of the whole story suggests, the New Testament, written by Jesus' first followers and friends, cannot be understood without the Old Testament. Jesus works to recreate the people of God, just as the ancient prophets of Israel did; but he extends the boundaries of the people of God to include all nations. The God who once made a 'covenant', an alliance, with the people of Israel, now makes a covenant with all who trust in God because of what Jesus says and does.

Often in Christian history, teachers and scholars have found that the words of the Bible may have a symbolic meaning beyond their surface meaning. If the Holy Spirit is involved in the writing of the Bible, this should not be surprising. But no Christian doctrine can be proved just by appealing to a symbolic meaning alone.

When the pastors and teachers of a Christian congregation deliver sermons, their main purpose is, or should be, to help believers understand the unity and harmony of the texts that have been read at an act of worship; and then to encourage them to live lives worthy of the good news that they have received.

## *Sacraments: baptism and Holy Communion*

All Christian public worship expresses first of all our gratitude that God has given his Spirit so that we can live by the power and love of Jesus the 'Anointed King' (which is what 'Christ' means). Admission to a full share in this worship is by baptism – a word which originally meant being dipped in water. According to Christian teaching, when water is poured over someone in the name of the Father, the Son and the Holy Spirit, that person's old life comes to an end – the life of slavery to disobedience – and the new life of the Spirit begins. When Christianity began, those baptized would be adults who had accepted belief in Jesus. As the Christian community grew and spread and families brought up their children to believe, it became more common for children to be baptized. In many churches, there is another ceremony performed by a bishop, 'confirmation', which is believed to complete or 'seal' what baptism does – though there is a fair amount of variety of teaching as to what exactly this might mean.

Practically all Christian communities meet for the ritual meal of bread and wine called the Holy Communion and sometimes referred to as the 'Eucharist' (from the Greek for thanksgiving) or 'Mass' (from the Latin for sending someone out to do his or her work). Many churches do this every day, most of them at least once a week. The ceremony has its origins in the action of Jesus the night before his crucifixion, when he ate his last supper with his disciples: as he said the blessing over the bread and wine at the table, he declared they were his 'body and blood'.

This language has often seemed strange or shocking. But its meaning must be looked for in the context of the Bible as a whole. The prophets of ancient Israel performed symbolic actions to show that God was about to do certain things. So Jesus, as he breaks the bread and shares the wine at supper, says that the bread broken and eaten shows what will happen to his body in his suffering, and the wine poured out represents his blood shed. In this suffering of his, though, God will be acting to free human beings from their slavery. The suffering Jesus endures will therefore be like food and drink for his friends – it will give life and strength. When they bless bread and wine in his name, the sharing of this food and drink will be an occasion for God's new life to enter into them afresh. Just as Jesus' human flesh and blood is the place where God's power and Spirit are at work, so in this bread and wine, blessed in his memory, the same power and Spirit are active.

But around this central idea many other images and concepts gather. The meal is a Christian version of the Passover meal of the Jews in which they remember how God led them out of slavery in Egypt. It's like the meal after a sacrifice in which something has been offered to God so as to make peace. It's like the meals Jesus shared with sinners and outcasts to show them that God was ready to welcome and forgive them. And it's like the meals that Jesus shared with his disciples after he had been raised from death. It's also the place where prayers are offered for all who need prayer. Because the Christian at Holy Communion stands especially close to Jesus, it's a time to bring our prayers into his prayer. Many Christians say that being at Holy Communion is being present in heaven while we are still on earth – because we are close to Jesus, praying with his voice, receiving his life. Many of the prayers used all over the Christian world talk about how at the Communion service we praise God alongside the angels and all the holy people of the past. When the community meets for Communion, it's part of the whole assembly of God's people, living and dead, on earth and in heaven.

## *The Christian life: love, justice and prayer*

Jesus declared at his last meal with the disciples that the love they had for each other should be a visible sign of the love between him and his heavenly Father – a love (as we saw earlier) that is something infinitely greater than any bond between two human individuals. In their behaviour, Christians are always meant to show love – not just a warm feeling for each other but a habit of seeing each other *as God sees human beings.* So love means readiness to forgive injuries and not to be self-righteous; it means being ready to give all we have for each other's welfare or healing; it means justice – treating everyone as equally God's creature, equally entitled to respect and service. Some think that Christian love is a 'soft' and vague thing; but if it doesn't include justice, it is meaningless. Generosity with our resources, whether by individual gift or by corporate or social care, is essential to Christian life. It's a scandal that so many historically Christian countries are often slow to give in this way to their own poor or to the poor of the rest of the world.

Our love must also be faithful love. We must be committed to each other and to service and justice in God's world, not following the feelings of a passing moment. This applies very directly to our human relationships. For Christians, marriage is a sign of God's promise and commitment to human beings and of Jesus' love for his people. This is why Christians have been uneasy about divorce – although many churches recognize that it's sometimes an unavoidable means of ending a failing or unjust or abusive relationship; they believe that sexual activity belongs properly in the context of publicly committed love and relationship. The principle of faithful love means also that the care of children is an essential aspect in a life of justice and goodness according to God's will. Tension between husband and wife, unfaithfulness, neglect or cruelty all have an impact on children as well as on partners and are therefore doubly tragic and destructive.

Although Christians put such a high value on forgiveness, they do not therefore reject the idea of just punishment applied by a lawful authority, including a non-Christian authority that acts with fairness and wisdom. In the history of the Church there have been different attitudes to whether it's right to go to war. Most have said that it can be justified on certain carefully defined conditions – if you are defending your people, if there is no possible alternative way of settling a dispute, if you can guarantee that innocent people will not be harmed or killed. But even on such conditions, there is a good deal of reservation in Christian tradition. Jesus in the Gospels opposes violence, even in self-defence, for any individual. But St Paul seems to allow that force can be used by rulers to restrain evildoers. There is always a sense, though, that force is second-best for the Christian, though it may be necessary in a threatening or unjust situation. Most Christians would now say that the history of the Crusades, for example, or the religious wars in Europe in the sixteenth and seventeenth centuries were serious betrayals of many of the central beliefs of the Christian faith. Any modern attempt to revive a crusading ideal or the language of 'holy war' is very unlikely indeed to be supported by most Christian believers today.

Last, it may be helpful to say a word about other kinds of Christian prayer. We have seen something of the meaning of what is said in public services. But Christians pray in private also. And in addition to praying for those in need and praying for forgiveness for their sins and giving thanks for blessings received, many Christians, since at least the third Christian century, have practised silent contemplation. They have disciplined their minds and bodies to be still so that the life of God may come into them more freely.

The tradition of monastic life has formed the background of much of this life of silence and adoration. Some are called, Christians believe, to live a life without marriage and property, under obedience to a common rule of life, so that in this austere and sacrificial environment they may more readily come into what many have called the 'repose' of silent prayer. Some too have written about how the journey into this silence may be a road of great suffering, a following of the suffering of Jesus in which familiar ideas and feelings drop away and we are left in dark and silence for long periods, as if God is purifying us of all pictures or ideas about him that are just the products of our own human minds. Christians who have experienced deep contemplative prayer often speak of the 'darkness' in which God lives – not because he doesn't want to communicate but because our minds and hearts are too small for him to enter fully, so that we experience God as challenging and overwhelming. But they also speak of light flooding the mind, like the light that flowed from the face of Jesus, according to the Gospels, when he was praying in the presence of his friends.

In summary, what the Christian hopes and prays for is that at the end he or she will be brought by the grace of God's Spirit to see the glory of God as it is shown in the face of Jesus, and to be so united with his prayer to the Father that we never fall away. All that the observer might see in a Christian meeting for worship is directed towards this. We seek to let the life that was alive in Jesus be alive in each one of us through the gift of God's Spirit. And we pray that this life will, through us, bring healing and peace to all the world.

# 2

## *What is faith?*

One of the great classics of Cambridge literature is Gwen Raverat's book, *Period Piece: A Cambridge childhood*. In it she gives a picture of her family; and among her uncles and aunts are several figures of ripe eccentricity. One uncle was absolutely convinced that whenever he left the room the furniture would rearrange itself while he was out. He was constantly trying to get back quickly enough to catch it in the act. Now, that is admittedly a rather extreme case of Cambridge eccentricity, but I suspect that it may ring one or two bells with some readers. How many of us, I wonder, as children had that haunting suspicion that perhaps rooms rearranged themselves when we were out? Wondered whether what we were seeing was what still went on when our backs were turned?

I want to begin this chapter by thinking about that aspect of our human being in the world which is puzzled, frustrated, haunted by the idea that maybe what we see isn't the whole story, and that maybe our individual perception is not the measure of all truth. Our ordinary perceptions of the world around are often jolted by grief or by joy. They're jolted in a way that leads us to want to say thank you, even if we don't know what or who to say thank you to. They're jolted when we don't know what to do with feelings for which we haven't yet got words or strategies. And that may be a long way from Gwen Raverat's uncle, but something of the same thing is going on. What if the world is not as tame as I'm inclined to think it is? What if my perception of things is not the measure of everything? Religious feeling and perception is based on a sense of human limit, human vulnerability if you will, and on the sense that to be human is not necessarily to be at the centre of things or to be in control of things as if we could have a kind of lighthouse vision that, circling about the entire scope of reality, lit up everything with an even light centred in *me*, my mind or my heart. What if, after all, I'm not at the centre of everything, but part of a vast and rich interweaving of points of view and kinds of energy mingling and shaping one another?

There are two things we can do with this question – one of them healthy and one of them not so healthy, one of them leading to terrible religion and one of them leading to faith. Terrible religion happens when we use our religious language, our religious stories, as a way of pretending to ourselves that we are after all in charge, that actually we really *are* the centre of things and our limits can be overcome. We believe we have access to absolute and infallible truth, to an even and just perspective on all things; we know what the world is really like and there's no more to be learned. It's terrible religion – but it's also a terrible form of humanism, especially when, even though it calls itself atheistic, it still clings to certain religious ideas (bad ones) by pretending that human beings can actually answer all the questions they set themselves and overcome all the limits that might threaten their power. And the trouble with bad religion, what makes it terrible, is that it's a way of teaching you to ignore what is real.

## *Seeing beyond the surface*

What about the 'healthy' response, then? I'm going to suggest that one of the tests of actual faith, as opposed to bad religion, is whether it *stops you ignoring things*. Faith is most fully itself and most fully life-giving when it opens your eyes and uncovers for you a world larger than you thought – and of course, therefore, a world that's a bit more alarming than you ever thought. The test of true faith is how much more it lets you see, and how much it stops you denying, resisting, ignoring aspects of what is real.

I used to know a very remarkable man who was for 26 years a senior consultant psychiatrist in Broadmoor Hospital – one of the more testing jobs in the system. He was also a great Shakespearean enthusiast, and one of his favourite lines was from *The Tempest* where Prospero says to Miranda, 'What seest thou else?' That, he said, was the question that kept him going as a psychiatrist. Confronted with horrendous and tragic situations, with people deeply disturbed and locked up in their own fantasies, he would have to ask himself repeatedly, 'What seest thou else?' What more is there to see? And for him, the enterprise of religious faith was about that *seeing more*, seeing that the world can't be fully seen just by one pair of eyes, that the world can't be fully seen even by the sum total of all pairs of human eyes, and seeing that the world has a dimension of real strangeness, a depth not sounded.

This is where religious faith most overlaps with art, but also with creative science. Creative science, remember, begins in that conviction that there is something *not seen*, there is something that I or we have been ignoring and it's time we stopped ignoring it. And the arts – poetry, sculpture, painting, drama – are all rooted in this feeling that the world is more than it shows to any one person in any one image at any one moment.

Religious faith, in other words, is a process of educating our vision and educating our passions: educating our vision so that we understand how to see that we *don't* see, how to see behind surfaces, the depth that we're not going to master; educating our passions in the sense of helping us to grow up 'humanly' in such a way that we don't take fright at this strangeness and mysteriousness and run away for all we're worth.

Faith is *inhabiting a larger world*. One of the problems of perception in our world today is that it so often looks as though faith leads you into a *smaller* world and makes smaller human beings, whereas those of us who try to live with and in it would want to say, actually, it's an immeasurably larger world. There's a famous sixteenth-century woodcut that you sometimes see reproduced in history books, which shows a human figure pushing its head through the firmament of heaven – the smooth, tidy firmament of heaven with the little stars on it. This person has pushed through it and is suddenly looking up into a sky that he's never seen before, packed with strange stars. That woodcut is often taken as a kind of image of what it felt like in the sixteenth century as the Renaissance unfolded, and people realized that the world was immeasurably bigger than they'd ever thought. It's quite often used as an image of resistance to traditional Christianity and religious authority. Yet I want to say that it ought to be an image of *authentic faith*, of a real understanding of what the tradition of religious practice does for you, pushing you through the smooth painted surface, out towards a sky with stars you've never seen.

## *The light of the gospel*

How does this play out specifically in the context of Christian faith? And why might that be worth taking seriously?

At this point I'm going to stop talking anything resembling philosophy for a bit and turn to the Gospel according to St John, and in particular to the story of how Jesus healed a blind man, found in John chapter 9.

> As he walked along, he saw a man blind from birth. His disciples asked him, 'Rabbi, who sinned, this man or his parents, that he was born blind?' Jesus answered, 'Neither this man nor his parents sinned; he was born blind so that God's works might be revealed in him. We must work the works of him who sent me while it is day; night is coming

when no one can work. As long as I am in the world, I am the light of the world.' When he had said this, he spat on the ground and made mud with the saliva and spread the mud on the man's eyes, saying to him, 'Go, wash in the pool of Siloam' (which means Sent). Then he went and washed and came back able to see. The neighbours and those who had seen him before as a beggar began to ask, 'Is this not the man who used to sit and beg?' Some were saying, 'It is he.' Others were saying, 'No, but it is someone like him.' He kept saying, 'I am the man.' But they kept asking him, 'Then how were your eyes opened?' He answered, 'The man called Jesus made mud, spread it on my eyes, and said to me, "Go to Siloam and wash." Then I went and washed and received my sight.' They said to him, 'Where is he?' He said, 'I do not know.'

They brought to the Pharisees the man who had formerly been blind. Now it was a sabbath day when Jesus made the mud and opened his eyes. Then the Pharisees also began to ask him how he had received his sight. He said to them, 'He put mud on my eyes. Then I washed, and now I see.' Some of the Pharisees said, 'This man is not from God, for he does not observe the sabbath.' But others said, 'How can a man who is a sinner perform such signs?' And they were divided. So they said again to the blind man, 'What do you say about him? It was your eyes he opened.' He said, 'He is a prophet.'

The Jews did not believe that he had been blind and had received his sight until they called the parents of the man who had received his sight and asked them, 'Is this your son, who you say was born blind? How then does he now see?' His parents answered, 'We know that this is our son, and that he was born blind; but we do not know how it is that now he sees, nor do we know who opened his eyes. Ask him; he is of age. He will speak for himself.' His parents said this because they were afraid of the Jews; for the Jews had already agreed that anyone who confessed Jesus to be the Messiah would be put out of the synagogue. Therefore his parents said, 'He is of age; ask him.'

So for the second time they called the man who had been blind, and they said to him, 'Give glory to God! We know that this man is a sinner.' He answered, 'I do not know whether he is a sinner. One thing I do know, that though I was blind, now I see.' They said to him, 'What did he do to you? How did he open your eyes?' He answered them, 'I have told you already, and you would not listen. Why do you want to hear it again? Do you also want to become his disciples?' Then they reviled him, saying, 'You are his disciple, but we are disciples of Moses. We know that God has spoken to Moses, but as for this man, we do not know where he comes from.' The man answered, 'Here is an astonishing thing! You do not know where he comes from, and yet he opened my eyes. We know that God does not listen to sinners, but he does listen to one who worships him and obeys his will. Never since the world began has it been heard that anyone opened the eyes of a person born blind. If this man were not from God, he could do nothing.' They answered him, 'You were born entirely in sins, and are you trying to teach us?' And they drove him out.

Jesus heard that they had driven him out, and when he found him, he said, 'Do you believe in the Son of Man?' He answered, 'And who is he, sir? Tell me, so that I may believe in him.' Jesus said to him, 'You have seen him, and the one speaking with you is he.' He said, 'Lord, I believe.' And he worshipped him. Jesus said, 'I came into this world for judgement so that those who do not see may see, and those who do see may become blind.' Some of the Pharisees

near him heard this and said to him, 'Surely we are not
blind, are we?' Jesus said to them, 'If you were blind, you
would not have sin. But now that you say, "We see", your
sin remains.'                                    (John 9.1–41)

I can't think of anywhere better to start in trying to spell
out a little bit of what the Christian story of *seeing* looks
and feels like. Notice how at the end of the story, Jesus
says to the Pharisees, 'But now that you say, "We see",
your sin remains.' Or as it might be translated, 'Because
you say we can see, you're stuck in your guilt.' In other
words, 'Only if you know you *can't* see can you find your
way.' It's one of those many startling paradoxes that occur
so often in John's Gospel. Jesus is addressing the religious
experts of the day and effectively saying, 'Your problem
is that you can't see that you can't see. You can't see what
it is that your habits, your status and your skill prevent
you engaging with.'

As the Gospel story unfolds, we get a clearer picture
of exactly what it is that these experts can't see. They
can't see the mechanisms that drive them: mechanisms
which lead them to be deeply afraid; mechanisms which
allow them to use violence to protect their safe and self-
justified positions; mechanisms that allow scapegoating,
that seek security at the expense of others. They can't see
all of that horrible, noisy, mechanical stuff going on inside
them and they are stuck with their guilt, says Jesus. They
don't know they can't see, and when vision is offered to
them, they run from it.

Well, that's not entirely surprising. Most of us, when
candid friends or even more candid enemies offer us

26

pictures of what we might really be like, are inclined to run. Very few human beings, whatever we may like to tell ourselves, have a natural taste for hearing the truth about themselves. When somebody says to you, 'Do you really want to know what I think?' the honest answer in most cases would be, 'Actually, no.'

So far, so obvious, you might say, and you might feel you don't entirely blame the religious experts in the Gospel for panicking at the prospect of being shown the mechanisms of their own fear and their own violence.

But what makes the difference in John's Gospel is that the story not only portrays a vision of yourself – a failing, ignorant, frightened self. The story of Jesus, as John tells it, also involves a vision of something else, which he calls *glory*: the radiance and the beauty that is at the root of everything. In the light of that radiance, you can't keep up the pretence of self-justification and self-protection. In the full light of that radiance, you can't be like the religious experts and say, 'I see, I've got it', and put the experience and the knowledge in a package in your pocket. Jesus' mission in this Gospel is described very clearly as the process of bringing that radical, radiant beauty to light in this world in such a way that only the most resolutely self-justifying and the most terminally terrified will want to resist.

Self-justification, fear and violence and all the rest of the package, these things become impossible in the light of that radiance, because according to the Gospel the radiance itself is the presence of an utter unselfishness at the heart of everything. What lies behind and beneath all reality, the Gospel says, is an action whereby the most full, powerful, resourceful reality you can imagine lets go of itself, makes over its own fullness of joy and life so that there may be life in another.

It begins in eternity; it fleshes itself out time and again in the world's history. The radiant beauty – the glory – of that gospel is the glory of a divine *letting-go*, and faced with that we're delivered, so we hope and pray, from the prison of violent self-justification. Why? Because if we are faced with that vision of an endless, unlimited unself-ishness, there is no one we have to persuade to love us, there is no hostile, defensive, cosmic tyrant somewhere over *there* that we have to placate.

All we have is an endless gift of unconditional love. All we have is what again in John's Gospel we see referred to as an unceasing *work*, an unceasing labour of giving life. At one point in the Gospel Jesus is defending the fact that he's breaking the Sabbath by healing somebody, and he says, 'My father is still at work, and I am still at work.' There is no interruption possible for this unselfish act of life-giving, healing restoration and affirmation.

We can perhaps recognize what a wonderful truth that would be, if it were *true*. And we might wonder how, precisely, such a vision could come to feel natural or possible for us. But that's where the story winds the ten-sion more and more tightly. As the story unfolds, we begin to see more clearly just how tightly we are locked into our self-deceptions. Gradually, as the story goes on, we see more and more deeply how and why human beings want to resist that double vision, the vision of their own fear and the vision of the love that overcomes it. And it seems as though fear wins. Jesus is condemned and executed. The human refusal to *see* finally means his death on the cross. But, says the Gospel, that death is itself a moment of glory yet again. Because there we see what a complete letting-go of the self in love actually looks like.

The symbol is lifted up before us, the symbol of a love with no conditions. The cross is itself: glory. The death of Jesus shows what is indestructible in the love of God, and the work goes on. God doesn't stop working, doesn't stop being this unselfish God because of our refusals. And so unbroken is that work that it goes on through and beyond the death of Jesus on the cross, and is shown in the resurrection after the great Sabbath of death.

Almost infinitely more could be said about the Gospel of John, one of the most inexhaustible texts in the whole of the Bible, but I hope I've said enough to show how much of it talks about faith as *seeing*. It's about that double vision of myself as frightened and potentially violent and of God as radiant, consistent and unceasingly creative. And that's what we're invited into in Christian faith: recognizing the self-deception, recognizing the glory. Indeed, in recognizing the glory, the radiance of an unceasing, selfless love, we are somehow enabled to face more courageously and more fully our own self-deceit.

The first two things that Jesus says in St John's Gospel are, 'What do you want?' and 'Come and see.' There couldn't really be a better introduction to faith. 'What do you want? Do you actually want to change your life? Do you actually want human wholeness? And if you do, come and see.' So the Gospel story begins not with an argument but with an invitation, an invitation to examine yourself and an invitation to be in a place where you can see something different: *'What seest thou else?'*

We're invited to take time with this story, because its claim – although fairly simple – is quite a devastating one. The claim that John's Gospel makes, indeed the whole of the Christian tradition makes, is that there is a single moment in the history of the human world where that world is completely transparent to the love that made it, where glory appears in a human face.

# 3

## *What difference does it make?*

Following on from what we saw in our brief look at the Gospel of John, I'd like now to invite you to consider what difference the Christian gospel might make to our lives and our world today.

We saw in the last chapter that the gospel says to us something like this: 'It's possible to live in a world where you can see your failure and your recurrent fears with clarity, but also to know that if you *want* healing, there are no conditions.' It's possible to live in a world where you can see these things and accept God's invitation to be healed, restored, forgiven and made whole. Stating it like that is, in some ways, still fairly general, so now I want to think a bit more about the states of mind, the attitudes and values that may flow from a faithful acceptance of such an invitation.

Faith, understood in this way, makes possible at least these three things. First of all, faith makes possible realism and perspective. It makes it possible for you to see yourself with, in the right sense, detachment; to see yourself not defensively and anxiously and not vainly and smugly either, but to see yourself in all kinds of roles that are often inglorious, yet always redeemable.

I see myself in faith as somebody who fails. I see myself in faith as somebody who's loved. I see myself as somebody who is called, summoned and entrusted with responsibility, and I see myself as failing again. And I see the possibility of restoration and new beginnings. And at no point in that cycle am I allowed to see myself as an ultimate waste of space. I can see myself realistically; I don't have to pretend I'm better than I am, I don't even have to pretend I'm worse than I am. I have to recognize my limits, my nature as a growing being and as a being that makes mistakes. And the message is 'Don't panic!'

Second, this sort of faith makes possible a way of valuing what's around you. If the world really is grounded in some unimaginable act of final unselfishness, then all that's there is *gift*. As you have a security in the presence of the source of all things, so everyone has. As you have a share in that eternal gift, so everyone has. You have been given space and time to grow into intimacy with holy love, and all around you is *gift*. The person next to you issues from divine giving, the material environment issues from divine giving; nothing is just *there*, everything and everyone is *given*.

And the third thing that grows out of this is that, if *that's* true, if indeed all things somehow flow from God's eternal giving, then the natural way to live as human beings in the world is in giving and receiving in a mutual intimacy. Not only intimacy with holy love at the centre of everything, but intimacy with one another – an intimacy that commits us to making one another more human in our relations with each other. And you could say, too, an intimacy with the whole world around us that allows the world to make us more human and that allows us to make the world more itself – an attitude of respect towards our environment that seems so inaccessible for 'advanced' societies.

Perspective and realism, evaluation of things as gift, a sense that we are called to committed intimacy in making each other more human: those three things that this kind of faith makes possible stand very firmly against their polar opposites, which I think you'll find familiar:

*Against emotional infantilism*: that utter lack of perspective that puts my immediate needs and the gratification of my immediate passions at the centre – which can show itself as greed, lust and irresponsibility and can equally show itself, as Jesus so often says, in censoriousness and hatred of the other.

*Against exploitative selfishness*: that desire to draw the whole human and non-human environment into the great hungry stomach of my ego, or of our collective human ego – an attitude that ravages and ruins the world around us.

*Against an attitude of calculation and suspicion in human relationships*: that cynical and corrosive outlook that assumes other individuals, other groups, other nations and the world at large are all there to be used as means to our own ends – and that that's how others see us.

Now, if you don't see these things around in our culture, I suspect you may not be looking very hard. It seems to me that those possibilities opened up by faith as *seeing* open the door to a way of resisting some of these most deeply destructive elements of the society we're in; the global culture which all of us in one way or another, in varying degrees, inhabit. And if we're talking about what difference it makes in relation to the world of politics, I would say that faith conceived in this way helps to make change in the direction of justice, change in the direction of reconciliation, truly possible.

## *What do you want? Come and see*

In this little book I've been trying to say something about the overall character of a religious commitment in our world, a character that is best expressed in terms of not only seeing but seeing that we're not seeing everything. I've tried to anchor that a bit in the way in which the basic Christian story is told in the Gospel of John, perhaps the most powerful of its expressions in the New Testament. I tried to suggest how seeing the world as John invites us to see it begins to grow in us a set of human responses that may become the material of resistance to what's most destructive in our world.

But, you might well say, that's all very attractive but is there any particular reason for thinking that it's true? And that's a question that everyone has to answer for himself or herself, precisely *because* it's not a knockdown argument we're talking about, but an invitation. We're not going to get to the point where someone can say, 'Here is the proof and any fool can see that that's how we should approach reality.'

That's why I mentioned earlier the significance of both science and art in understanding faith. There's an element of risk involved in all our significant commitments. The scientist embarking on a new direction of experimentation is taking risks that will lead to a whole series of non-confirmations of a theory before, finally, perhaps something clicks. But this in turn will set off a new train of questions. And then, when we're faced with a great work of the imagination, a poem, film, play or novel, it's not as though the author comes to us and says, 'I can prove to you that this is how reality is.' The author is saying something a lot more like Jesus at the beginning of John's Gospel: 'Come and see. Discover what you can see by standing here with me.' And if by standing here it's possible to see what otherwise I can't see, I may perhaps at least begin to suspect that there is truth to be seen from this perspective, not just mine alone.

To come out of a production of *King Lear* shaken, uncertain and disturbed is to know that I've seen something I'd rather not have seen. There's more than I had thought. Is *King Lear* true? Well, it's not a true story about ancient Britain, but it's a true story about the world we're in. Uncomfortable because true, because it puts me in touch with things I might feel more comfortable not knowing. So when that question arises, 'Is all that true?' my answer is that, if by standing where Jesus invites you to stand you see more than you would otherwise see, if you see a world larger than you thought you inhabited, you have at least to ask yourself, 'Is not *this* a reality?' and perhaps also to ask 'Am I afraid of this reality?' And if this even *might* be the truth, might be the grain of the real world, where do I want to put myself?

The story of Jesus as it's presented to us in the Gospel of John and the rest of the Christian Bible is unlike any other in that it holds together, inseparably, that two-fold vision I've spoken of: the overwhelming reality of divine gift, the terrifying reality of human self-deceit and fear. The story of Jesus as it's told there is not just an epiphany – a revelation of glory and no more – and it's not just a commandment or a set of instructions dropped down from heaven. It's a manifestation of radiant beauty that lands in our world in the form of a profound moral challenge, because it's a revelation of active love that dissolves fear.

There are all kinds of experiences, epiphanies, manifestations of the holy. You may know a wonderful poem of Rilke's about an archaic Greek statue. It ends with the memorable lines 'There is no place where you are unseen. You have to change your life.' Now, that sense of a revelation which invites you to change, that's *part* of what the gospel is about, but it's even more, because the revelation is itself a revelation of an action of love into which you are invited to come, with which you are invited to cooperate. *Come and see.* See whether it's possible for you to let go of that anxious and destructive self in the face of a promise of radiant beauty; to be made alive in this way.

Across the human world many ways are proposed for human healing, for the restoration of humanity, but the claim of the gospel is quite simply that here in this encounter with this person we are brought to what the Gospel of St John itself describes as a secure and eternal place, 'in the bosom of the Father', next to the heart of all things, the place where fear becomes meaningless.

And so, in considering what Christianity is all about and what faith in Christ really means, we are left with a question and an invitation: 'What do you want?' says Jesus; and then, 'Come and see.' There are also those other profoundly resonant words in the Gospels which Jesus speaks to his friends: 'Launch out into the deep.' Understand that your life lies in the not knowing as well as the knowing; your life lies in understanding your limits; your life lies in letting go and allowing love, reconciliation and intimacy to flourish; your life lies in aligning yourself with that energy of creative gift which sustains the entire universe.

# Further reading

Here is a short list of books that can guide you further in your exploration of the topics discussed in this book. All are published by SPCK and are available from bookshops or from www.spck.org.uk.

Alister McGrath, *Faith and the Creeds: Christian belief for everyone* (2013)

Keith Ward, *Christianity: A guide for the perplexed* (2007)

Rowan Williams, *Being Christian: Baptism, Bible, Eucharist, prayer* (2014)

Rowan Williams, *Meeting God in Mark* (2014)

Tom Wright, *Simply Christian* (2011)

Tom Wright, *Simply Good News: Why the gospel is news and what makes it good* (2015)